LA 2000+

NEW ARCHITECTURE IN *LOS ANGELES*

LA 2000+

NEW ARCHITECTURE IN LOS ANGELES

JOHN LEIGHTON CHASE

THE MONACELLI PRESS

First published
in the United States of America
in 2006 by
The Monacelli Press, Inc.
611 Broadway
New York, NY 10012

LIBRARY OF CONGRESS CATALOGING-IN-PUBLICATION DATA
Chase, John, 1953–
  L.A. 2000+ : new architecture in Los Angeles /
John Leighton Chase.
    p. cm.
  ISBN 1-58093-171-5
  1. Architecture—California—Los Angeles—21st century.
  2. Los Angeles (Calif.)—Buildings, structures, etc. I. Title:
L.A. 2000 plus. II. Title.
  NA735.L55C45 2006
  720.9794'94090511—dc22

                            2005034337

Printed and bound in Italy

Designed by Green Dragon Office, Los Angeles,
Lorraine Wild and Stuart Smith

CONTENTS

STUDIO PALI FEKETE ARCHITECTS, SOMIS HAY BARN

INTRODUCTION

Los Angeles is often portrayed as a place of unbridled chaos, where thoughtlessly made buildings are thrown together in ad hoc relationships. It is also blithely assumed to be a tabula rasa for designers—no history, no culture, no restrictions, no structure, and clients who are up for almost anything. Neither assumption is entirely true, of course. It would be more accurate to say that Los Angeles is a place where architects have more opportunity to introduce new forms than they would in a city like Washington, D.C., for example, with its neoclassical traditions. But even in Los Angeles, those opportunities are limited mostly to smaller commissions, and to the chagrin of local architecture critics, the general public often prefers period-revival architecture—much of it badly, halfheartedly executed. The miracle is that there is any measurable body of notable modernist work here at all.

Still, if Los Angeles is not the playpen for architectural innovation it is sometimes made out to be, it *is* a large enough city with enough design "savy" residents—many of them in creative fields—to support a niche market for high-art, avant-garde architecture. This book presents a sampling of that work, all of it completed by Los Angeles architects in Los Angeles since 2000. (The criteria for inclusion ruled out a number of important local firms that do much of their work elsewhere, such as Moore Ruble Yudell.) The thirty firms included in these pages by no means constitute the last word on the current architecture in the region, but they do represent a wide range of architects, in terms of both their ages and the size of their practices—from small, new firms such as null. lab and Predock_Frane to older, more established offices run by architects who have enjoyed long and distinguished careers, such Barton Myers, Craig Hodgetts, and Ming Fung. There are no large corporate offices represented, however, because they have not produced much interesting work here in the last five years. In Los Angeles, as in so many other cities, these firms usually receive the biggest commissions, which are often too constrained by politics and/or conservative clients to produce true works of architecture.

It is no coincidence that of the thirty architects, the three most formally adventurous are also the most celebrated: Thom Mayne of Morphosis, Frank Gehry, and Eric Moss have received more press than any of the other architects because of the highly original nature of their work. Gehry, especially, is a major figure on an international scale, so ubiquitous that he has even appeared on an episode of *The Simpsons*. Like Frank Lloyd Wright, he is now an über-architect whose very name and persona have come to symbolize the profession of architecture to the larger world. His office has been a training ground for many of the city's young architects, and some of them have been directly influenced by his work. Randall Stout, one former employee whose Blair Graphics project is included here, breaks up the building mass into individual components in a move that is clearly Gehry-derived. Mayne's office has served a similar function; his influence can be seen in the splayed and inflected forms of Michele Saee's Linnie House and null.lab's Bobco Metals Office.

But Los Angeles has a large and varied talent pool, and the city's architecture is more than the work of a few superstars and their disciples. In fact, most of the architects in this book were not directly influenced by Gehry, Mayne, or Moss. They are all, however, modernists—although what constitutes a modernist in the twenty-first century is the subject of debate, as he or she may or may not be concerned with the rationalist project of methodical ordering that held sway during much of the twentieth century. Random patterning, splintering, fragmentation, gestural components, and curved, morphing forms are hallmarks of some current architectural production—and a few of the projects shown here. Gehry's Walt Disney Concert Hall combines both rational and nonrational systems of ordering, its stainless panel sculptural form coexisting with a rectilinear wing and base on the south and east. Other projects that employ similar design logic include the Bobco Metals Office, Blair Graphics, Eric Moss's Beehive, and Daly Genik's South Campus for Art Center.

SPARANO + MOONEY ARCHITECTURE, ARCADIA HISTORICAL MUSEUM

If one accepts that these architects are all modernist, then the next logical question is whether there is some particular quality that identifies them as distinctly Angeleno. In other words, does regionalism still exert an influence on avant-garde architecture in the twenty-first century? Thom Mayne famously dismissed the idea as "preposterous" nearly fifteen years ago at a symposium held in conjunction with the Angels & Franciscans exhibition at 65 Thompson Street in New York, and that would seem to have become increasingly true in the post-Internet world.

In the early 1990s, however, the critic Charles Jencks contended that there was, in fact, a Los Angeles school of architecture, and that it was characterized by a collision of disparate parts visible in various new buildings throughout the city. According to Jencks, it was inspired by the vitality and cacophony of the urban environment, or the "heteropolis," as he called it. One has only to look at the architecture represented here to see that this simplistic construct is no longer entirely applicable (if indeed it ever was). The work in this book is often characterized by unity of conception and execution: buildings like John Friedman and Alice Kimm's Los Angeles Design Center and Lorcan O'Herlihy's Jai House are serenely composed, all the elements working together, as is Josh Schweitzer's Congregation Kol Ami, a composition of nested stucco boxes that harks back to Frank Gehry's 1965 Danziger Studio in Hollywood. Moreover, many of the architects were trained or have practiced outside Los Angeles, and the formal themes they explore—for example, the idea of the permeable screen wall in Sparano + Mooney's museum in Arcadia—can be found in the work of architects throughout the world. Still, Jencks's assertion has a certain amount of merit. Craig Hodgetts's library is undeniably an assemblage of very diverse pieces, and Clive Wilkinson's office interior has a similarly collaged appearance. But while Jencks interpreted this aesthetic as a literal reflection of the diversity of the city, it seems more likely to be the result of the creative license and freedom that flourish here. Put simply, it's a formal preference for mixing rather than matching, a tradition that originated with Frank Gehry, among others.

NULL.LAB, BOBCO METALS OFFICE

The box and the steel frame also emerge as significant elements in much of this work. They may not be unique to the region, but they do have important precedents in the rationalist strain of Southern California modernism. Local architects such as Richard Neutra and the post-and-beam Case Study House designers used regular structural bays and exposed framework to create a strong, almost classical order. Studio Pali Fekete Architects' Somis Hay Barn, a post–Craig Ellwood temple of exposed construction, follows in this tradition, as do Barton Myers's 9350 Civic Center Drive and Frederick Fisher's Erburu Gallery.

Other buildings in this collection have a more ambiguous genealogy. Koning Eizenberg's Plummer Park Community Center combines a traditional ranch house–style pitched roof and open ceiling with starkly modern elements such as a long band of butt-joined glazing set into a white stucco box. Studioworks's Armenian School is an idiosyncratic juxtaposition of an airy library floating on stilts with a gymnasium buried in the ground.

Some buildings in the book do seem to share a particularly vital spirit, a special joie de vivre fostered by the fertile diversity of the city. This kinship may be the result of architects dealing with similar problems and materials, and working within the same zeitgeist. Godfredsen-Sigal made the most out of the opportunity for hedonism offered by the Hustler Casino, presenting American icon Larry Flynt with exuberant forms, lighting, patterns, and colors. Tolkin & Associates bestowed a playful, decorative quality on the Saladang Song restaurant without compromising the underlying rigor of the design. Both projects take advantage of the benign Southern California climate by providing outdoor spaces that accommodate programmatic needs: in the case of the former, a smoking area at the heart of the casino; in the latter, a dining terrace.

If the city's unique spirit is evident in a number of these projects, it doesn't seem unreasonable to expect that its ethnic diversity might emerge as an influence as well. After all, the city's single most notable characteristic may be its growing immigrant population—some 36 percent of Los Angeles County residents are now foreign-born. But this ethnic and cultural diversity is not, for the most part, reflected in the city's buildings: Korean-American residents do not live in buildings that somehow look Korean; Mexican-American residents do not live in buildings that look Mexican. Language, food, and religion are easier to import than architecture, and most immigrants have chosen to work with the vernacular of their new city. The urban fabric and ethnic populations may both be diverse, but the two kinds of diversity do not appear to be linked. The one exception to this seeming aesthetic disconnect is graphics. There is no question that immigrant—and particularly Latino—cultures have introduced stronger colors and a vibrant convention of representational graphics to the city. Mark Mack's Abbot Kinney Artist Lofts make use of this strong color, as do Koning Eizenberg's community center, Godfredsen-Sigal's casino, and Rios Clementi Hale's prototype classrooms for the Los Angeles Unified School District (which incorporate representational images that recall the graphics on immigrant storefronts).

There are other common concerns that can be observed in these projects, although none of them is particularly regional in nature. One is the now commonplace use of the computer as drawing tool and form generator. Every medium suggests its own aesthetic possibilities, and the computer's ability to create complex, nonorthogonal forms has had an international influence. Among the projects collected here, Neil Denari's Endeavor Talent Agency, in particular, makes a statement about the computer as a generator of design vocabularies as well as a form of representation, commenting on the ambiguity and equivalence of wall, floor, and ceiling planes as they merge and slide into each other.

MACK ARCHITECT(S), ABBOTT KINNEY ARTIST LOFTS

Another issue is that of sustainability—the effort to design buildings that make the fewest possible demands on the resources of the planet. Although there is no such thing as a truly sustainable architecture, there are measures architects can take to limit the amount of energy and resources it takes to build, inhabit, and maintain a building, and to decrease its relative toxicity, both for its inhabitants and the world at large. Pugh + Scarpa's Solar Umbrella House and Morphosis's Caltrans Headquarters both show a concern for these issues, incorporating large expanses of solar panels as key design elements.

The city's biggest need, however, is for sustainability on an urban scale—development that places land uses in proximity to each other, maximizing housing density and the thereby minimizing use of the automobile. Unfortunately, the most accomplished new architecture is not always accompanied by equally accomplished urban design. The Walt Disney Concert Hall has a beautiful garden, but it is on the roof—a far cry from the street-level garden originally proposed, which would have acted as a true outdoor room. And the Caltrans building's blind east and south facades contribute nothing to the public realm—in fact, they are textbook examples of how *not* to design facades.

Worse still, there is much building that simply isn't architecture at all. In a city with a reputation as a breeding ground for adventurous architects, why is the Walt Disney Concert Hall the only major Frank Gehry building constructed within the past few years? While it would be nice to trumpet a new era of enlightened design, that is sadly not the case. High-art modernism remains a boutique genre, with few exceptions—among them the Disney and Caltrans buildings and Eric Moss's work in Culver City. There is evidence of a new interest in design among some sectors of the public: the renewed popularity of mid-century modernism in Palm Springs and the city's massive library- and school-building campaigns are hopeful signs. Hodgetts + Fung's library is one example of an imaginative and fully realized work of architecture that emerged from the latter effort.

But there is a long way to go. The single-family house has become unaffordable for all but the wealthiest Angelenos. The city is struggling to deal with enormous population growth, beyond what can possibly be accommodated in new single-family houses. There are several included in this book because the region continues to be famous for them, and they serve an important role in architectural culture, providing a source of commissions for smaller firms and an opportunity to experiment. But projects such as Roschen Van Cleve's Sunset and Vine building, which incorporates a mix of uses at a high density, are the only real way to house

the city's growing population and solve its traffic woes. Others in the same vein include the West Hollywood Gateway by the Jerde Partnership, a retail complex that will ultimately include some three hundred units of housing, and Daly Genik's Art Center building, which is part of a new urban infill campus with housing in Pasadena. (On a smaller scale, the Saladang Song restaurant and the Pasadena Museum of California Art both include residences for the owners on the premises.)

It should be noted that some 90 percent of the projects in this book are object, rather than infill, buildings, a characteristic that makes them easily distinguishable from avant-garde buildings in other parts of the country, particularly on the East Coast. Los Angeles is increasingly becoming a dense city, but there is still more latitude for architects here than in eastern cities where buildings reinforce traditional street walls. The question this raises is whether the kind of high-density, mixed-use development the city needs will come at the expense of the excitement and individual interest generated by buildings like the ones in this book. The answer is anyone's guess.

Nevertheless, the most important architectural issue at the beginning of the twenty-first century is not that of aesthetics but of the remaking of the city. The further densification of Los Angeles presents avant-garde architects with a challenge to create urban infill that responds to an increasingly urbanized context with the spirit of innovation for which the region is celebrated. At the turn of the twenty-first century, the city continues to be an exciting venue for an extraordinary number of talented architects at various stages of their careers. But it remains to be seen if architectural patronage will evolve to allow smaller, more creative architecture firms with stronger design ideas to have a bigger slice of the pie. As the architects represented in this book demonstrate, the talent is out there.

DALY GENIK ARCHITECTS, ART CENTER COLLEGE OF DESIGN SOUTH CAMPUS

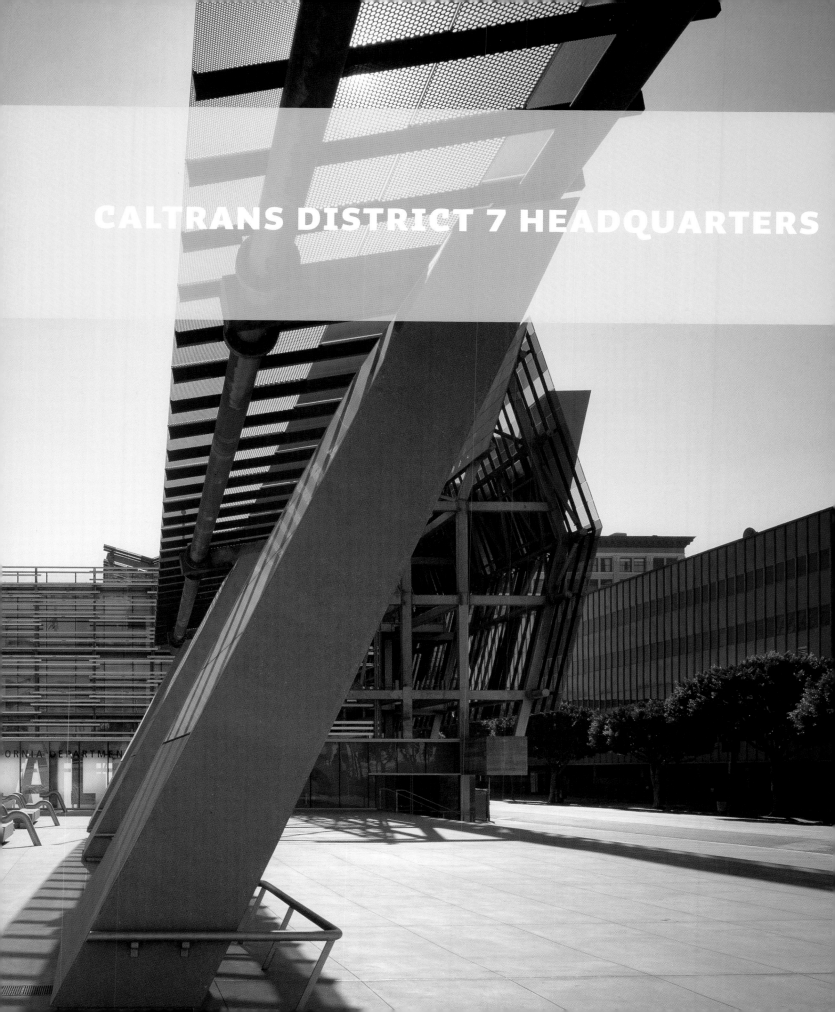

CALTRANS DISTRICT 7 HEADQUARTERS

MORPHOSIS   **DOWNTOWN LOS ANGELES, 2004**

The California State Department of Transportation District 7 Headquarters is the most controversial building constructed in Los Angeles in the past twenty years. To some, it's one of a handful of new landmarks breathing life into downtown, a welcoming structure that draws the public in with a sequence of gestures on its western ground-level facade, which has a public plaza with an amphitheater and a triple-height canopy. Others see it as the biggest, baddest, blankest building in all of downtown, the minimalism of its upper stories with their slit-like openings projecting a defended image. Most people agree, however, that the building is impressive by virtue of its sheer size, if nothing else—because of the minimalist cladding of the thirteen-story main block, it has a physical presence as arresting as that of the Hoover Dam.

CALTRANS DISTRICT 7 HEADQUARTERS

CALTRANS DISTRICT 7 HEADQUARTERS

The main facade, which faces west, receives the harshest sun exposure, so its conventional glass curtain wall is almost entirely covered by perforated aluminum screens, recalling Richard Neutra's nearby 1962 Hall of Records. Like the giant metal louvers in Neutra's building, which ratchet into open or closed positions depending on the time of day, the screens at Caltrans are controlled by a computer according to changing sun angles. The south side of the building is also technologically innovative, clad entirely in photovoltaic cells. In fact, whole sections of the building appear to be in motion, as if the design were in the process of composing itself. One these moving elements is a huge glass-and-metal beam-like feature that protrudes from the northern facade, projecting to the west of the building.

Supergraphics are another important design element: the supersized numerals of the street address are an integral part of the western façade, and an outsized Caltrans sign is incorporated into the pedestrian plaza. The four-story outdoor lobby is also animated by Keith Sonnier's neon artwork *Motordom*, inspired by taillights on a freeway.

CALTRANS DISTRICT 7 HEADQUARTERS

DUARTE HIGH SCHOOL

OSBORN ARCHITECTS   **DUARTE, 2003**

Although the big move in this project is the praying mantis–like profile of the entrance canopy and its supergraphic letters spelling out the school's name, the building has considerable architectural merit in and of itself—which is not always the case in the post–*Learning from Las Vegas* era, when designers often rely on huge signs as a substitute for architecture. The drama extends to the school's interior, where the double-height entrance corridor is lined with glass walls that have plaster-infill patterns, maintaining the sense of openness that defines the outdoor walkway.

    The architects gutted some of the existing classrooms and repurposed them as a new administration building. They also added a library, along with a roof that floats on I-beams, allowing for clerestory windows. In the classroom wings, an integrated concrete post-and-beam structure forms the building's spine, tapering at one end. The library fans out from a central reading room and a study room situated on either side of a set of vertical and diagonal steel beams.

DUARTE HIGH SCHOOL

BOBCO METALS OFFICE

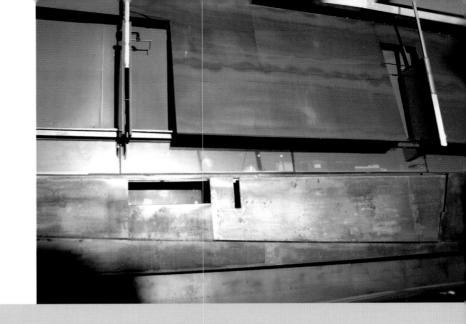

NULL.LAB

Iranian-born architects Arshia Mahmoodi and Reza Begherzadeh envisioned their design for Bobco, a metal wholesaler with a huge yard and warehouse, as a reflection of the noir, dystopian character of downtown Los Angeles. Of any recent project in the city, the Bobco Metals Office comes closest to being the realization of a computer-generated cyberspace. Using a hard-edged vocabulary and metals scrounged from the company's treasure chest, the architects revamped the existing headquarters into a five-thousand-square-foot metal interior terraced in three levels—the showroom on the first floor, the sales office on the second, and the management offices on the top level. Because all the elements read as roughly equivalent in importance and scale, the space resembles a landscape of jagged, hurtling planes, rather than a conventional work space with walls and a ceiling.

BOBCO METALS OFFICE

The typical disparity between the pristine photography of a just-completed project and the reality of the disorder and wear that eventually ensue as the result of life in the workaday world could be especially pronounced with this space, given the nature of the wholesale metals business. How does it look with clutter? How will it look as it ages? Modern architecture doesn't always hold up to scrutiny on either count. Nonetheless, this design's exploded space expresses life and movement, and it may well endure habitation and the passage of time better than most.

BOBCO METALS OFFICE

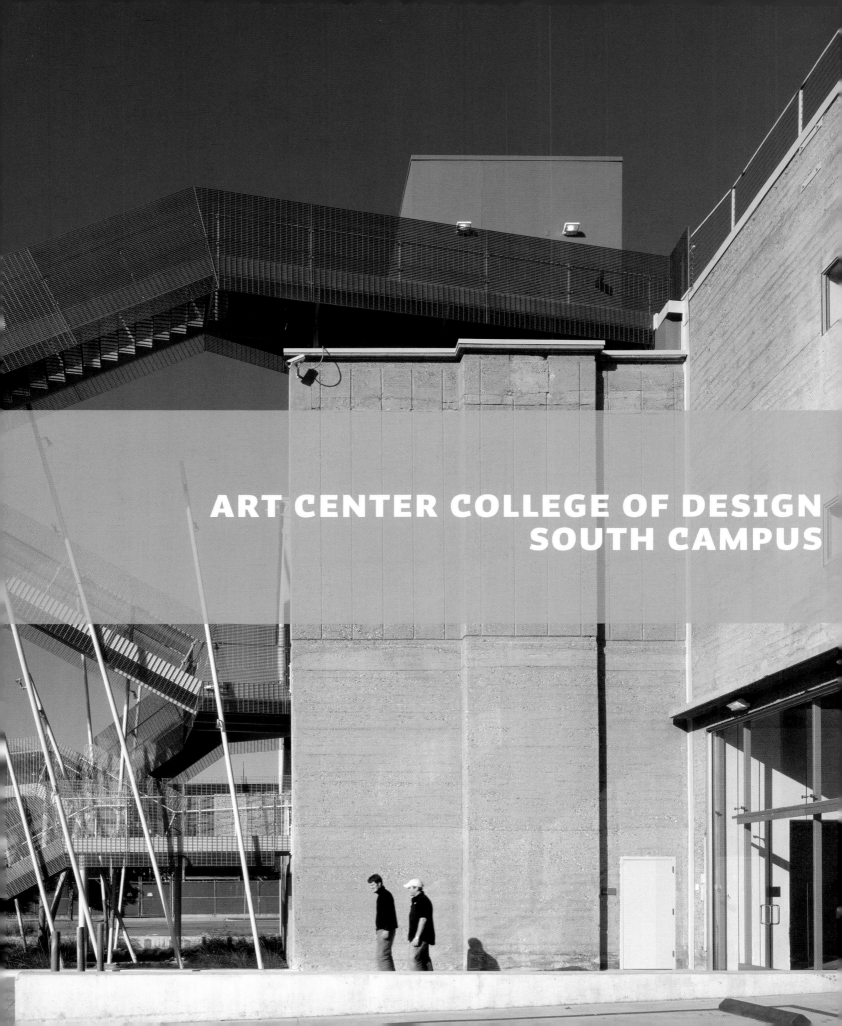

ART CENTER COLLEGE OF DESIGN
SOUTH CAMPUS

DALY GENIK ARCHITECTS   **PASADENA, 2004**

Art Center's original campus in West Pasadena was an icon of Southern California modernism, designed by Craig Ellwood and built in 1977 as a giant box-truss bridge across a ravine—a temple on a hill. Its new annex represents a radical departure from the school's history of isolationism, taking advantage of the deaccession of industrial buildings integrated into the urban fabric along the border between Pasadena and South Pasadena.

The first piece of a larger complex, the ninety-thousand-square-foot Graduate Fine Arts and Public Education Building houses galleries, studios, a sixteen-thousand-square-foot performance space, and facilities for digital design, model making, photography

ART CENTER COLLEGE OF DESIGN
SOUTH CAMPUS

and film, painting, drawing, woodworking, and printing. Constructed by Caltech in conjunction with aircraft companies such as Douglas, the building had a twenty-foot supersonic wind tunnel that was originally used for aircraft testing in the 1950s, which accounts for its unusual floor plan as well as its lack of windows and street access.

The architects intervened as little possible in the interior; on the exterior, however, they made major cuts, puncturing the roof to create perforations that bring light into the windowless studios and classrooms, and accommodate skylights. Designed in collaboration with the graphic design guru Bruce Mau, Ove Arup structural engineers, and Foiltec technicians, these sculptural skylights provide a lovely counterpoint to the bulk of the building, as does the metal stair at the south end of the building, which rests on a pickup-stick forest of reed-thin steel poles.

ART CENTER COLLEGE OF DESIGN
SOUTH CAMPUS

ART CENTER COLLEGE OF DESIGN
SOUTH CAMPUS

ROSE AND ALEX PILIBOS
ARMENIAN SCHOOL

STUDIOWORKS   **EAST HOLLYWOOD, 2003**

In their new gymnasium and library for the Rose and Alex Pilibos Armenian School in East Hollywood, one of the most diverse multiethnic communities in Southern California, Robert Mangurian and Mary-Ann Ray created two distinct structures. The pale turquoise, cement-board-clad library appears to float over a field of skinny poles and elliptical columns, hovering over the edge of the gymnasium roof below. The gymnasium is carved into the ground to insulate it, since the building is not air-conditioned. A standard-issue prefab structure with custom modifications, it was designed in collaboration with engineers at the Butler Manufacturing Company's Visalia office and factory. Its large, high-ceilinged volume is lit by glowing translucent panels and enclosed by outsize pivoting doors.

ROSE AND ALEX PILIBOS
ARMENIAN SCHOOL

ROSE AND ALEX PILIBOS
ARMENIAN SCHOOL

The library is housed in a boat-shaped structure, and its interior is sheathed in a plywood skin that integrates the bookshelves, computer desks, benches, and display areas. Strategically placed windows capture views of the Hollywood Hills and the Griffith Observatory, as well as a nearby Armenian church. Nautically inspired stairways and bridges connect the two structures to the existing buildings.

ROSE AND ALEX PILIBOS
ARMENIAN SCHOOL

WALT DISNEY CONCERT HALL

GEHRY PARTNERS   **DOWNTOWN LOS ANGELES, 2003**

The Walt Disney Concert Hall is to Los Angeles what the 1957–73 Jørn Utzon Opera House is to Sydney. The form of the Sydney hall may be more regular and its harbor location more propitious, but the Los Angeles building displays the same free-form vocabulary that made Gehry's waterside Guggenheim Museum in Bilbao an icon. (In fact, the museum in Bilbao was designed in 1991, three years after the symphony hall, but it was completed five years earlier and thus came to be seen as the archetypal Gehry building.)

The project began with a $50 million gift from Walt Disney's widow, Lillian, which financed a limited competition between Gehry, Hans Hollein, Gottfried Böhm, and James Stirling. Construction started on Gehry's winning scheme but was halted in 1994, after the parking garage base was built: the project had gone way over budget, from $110 million to an estimated $264 million, and the project architects hired to work with Gehry were having trouble producing construction documents from his three-dimensional computer renderings. A campaign by press and local architects, led by Mayor Richard Riordan and the philanthropist Eli Broad, raised an additional $187 million. The final obstacle was overcome after Lillian Disney's daughter, Diane Disney Miller, threatened to take the Disney name off the project unless Gehry was given permission to execute his own construction drawings, thus guaranteeing him the ability to control the design of the finished building. Construction resumed in 2000, and three years later the landmark building was complete.

WALT DISNEY CONCERT HALL

The site slopes to the east and the south, exposing the orthogonal lines of the building's stone-clad base. The entire building was originally meant to be covered in limestone, but 3/16-inch-thick wire-brushed steel was substituted to save money and allow the architect to create stronger, compound curves. A grand stair sweeps up from the northwest corner of the building, at the intersection of Grand Avenue and First Street, to the lobby. Stairs at the northeast and southwest corners lead to the roof garden. At the heart of the building is the 2,265-seat auditorium—a stunning space with curved, pillow-like wooden walls and a gently draping wooden ceiling.

WALT DISNEY CONCERT HALL

BLAIR GRAPHICS

RANDALL STOUT ARCHITECTS

RANDALL STOUT ARCHITECTS   **SANTA MONICA, 2000**

A small, simple building with a richly developed sense of sculptural form, this project is a rare example of a built work in Los Angeles that clearly exhibits the influence of Frank Gehry's current vocabulary of morphing volumes. While Blair Graphics is a modest project, and Gehry's best-known recent project, the Walt Disney Concert Hall, is a blockbuster, both share the idea that structure should follow form; in each case, the abstract vocabulary is as independent as possible from the usual constraints of building. It's an aesthetic that is appropriate for the client, Blair Graphics, which has transformed itself from an old-fashioned blueprint and photo-reproduction shop into a contemporary electronic-information-and-image-processing firm.

The abstraction of the building's galvanized metal canopy is emphasized by the simplicity of its backdrop. The facade itself was simplified with frameless glass windows; face brick further unifies it. Two faceted forms create a focal point in the lobby—one growing from the floor, the other from the roof—barely touching, like stalactite and stalagmite.

BLAIR GRAPHICS

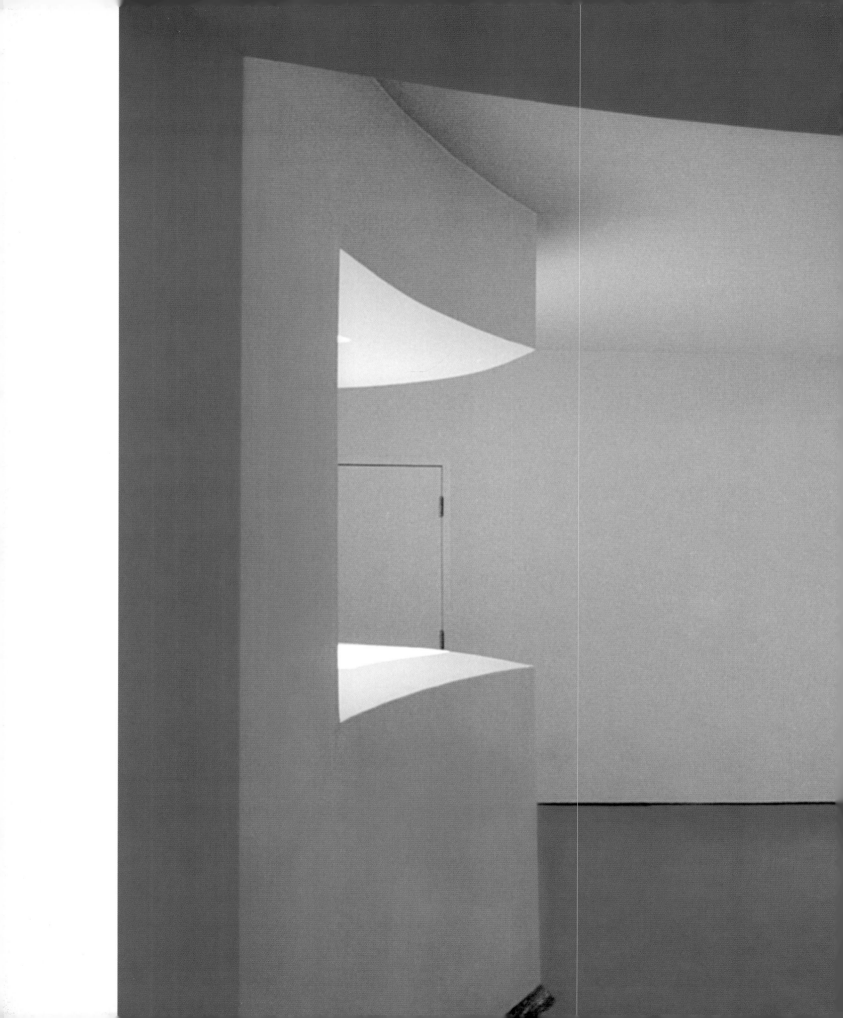

**PASADENA MUSEUM
OF CALIFORNIA ART**

PASADENA MUSEUM
OF CALIFORNIA ART

MDA JOHNSON FAVARO

For a pair of clients who wanted to start their own museum in downtown Pasadena and live in an apartment above it, architects Steve Johnson and Jim Favaro conceived a design that incorporates a traditional Spanish-colonial-revival wall, as a contextual response to the site and a reference to the city's architectural heritage. By cutting into and folding the wall into multiple layers, the architects fashioned what they called "drapery folds," creating a building that is simultaneously modern and traditional.

The design was dictated by budgetary constraints, which meant that most of the ground floor had to be devoted to parking. To compensate, the architects lavished attention on the remaining part of the ground floor reserved for pedestrians and the stairs to the galleries on the second floor, crafting a curvilinear staircase, an oculus, and curving walls that direct visitors to the main gallery space. On the third floor, the owner's five-thousand-square-foot residence shares space with a subsidiary gallery and a roof terrace.

ENDEAVOR TALENT AGENCY

NEIL M. DENARI ARCHITECTS   **BEVERLY HILLS, 2004**

A Piranesi-like figure, Neal Denari has a reputation as a leading auteur of mysterious cyberspace designs. In his second built work in Los Angeles—following the impressive 2002 L.A. Eyeworks store on Melrose—he has employed that sensibility to create suitably glamorous offices for the Endeavor Talent Agency. The company wanted to project an adventurous image that would help distinguish it from its chief competitor, industry giant Creative Artists Agency, which inhabits a majestic I. M. Pei building nearby.

ENDEAVOR TALENT AGENCY

The office's drama comes from the play of light over white walls, ceilings, and terrazzo floors, all of which have rounded corners, like contemporary appliances or computers, producing aerodynamic forms and continuous surfaces. The box is not so much broken as melted together and sliced apart. There are breaks in the walls in unexpected places: in an asymmetrical hall, one wall bends out at a right angle to the floor while the opposite one stops short of the ceiling, allowing light to pass through. The interior is divided into four color zones—magenta, cyan, orange, and green—and graphics include giant blowups of television images, a commentary on the power of electronic media.

FOOTE, CONE & BELDING
WORLDWIDE HEADQUARTERS

FOOTE, CONE & BELDING
WORLDWIDE HEADQUARTERS

CLIVE WILKINSON ARCHITECTS   **IRVINE, 2001**

Transforming this onetime heart-valve factory into ad agency offices presented something of a challenge for the architects, particularly because the original building consisted of two very different kinds of spaces: an open, double-height warehouse and conventional, closed-in research laboratories. The solution involved inventing a nautical theme to unify the two distinct spaces into a single creative office. What the architects referred to as "floating structures" linked by "a jetty-like bridge" were inserted in the warehouse to accommodate conventional offices adjacent to the open work areas. Conversely, double-height, dock-like spaces were dropped into the laboratory side.

A wide corridor leads from the entrance past a red, two-story display wall to the office area, where public meeting rooms are housed in steel-faced structures; one of them, a raised boardroom, is a grotto-like enclosure with twenty-foot-high walls decorated with 142 surfboards. An open meeting area on top of the management offices houses two structures known as "Ping" and "Pong": the former holds speakers and TV monitors, and the latter, audiovisual equipment. The two are fronted with whiteboard so they can be used as work surfaces. Textures vary widely through the building, reflecting the controlled chaos of the creative process: one conference room is all wood, with large, movable shutters; another is defined solely by free-form, tentlike dividers.

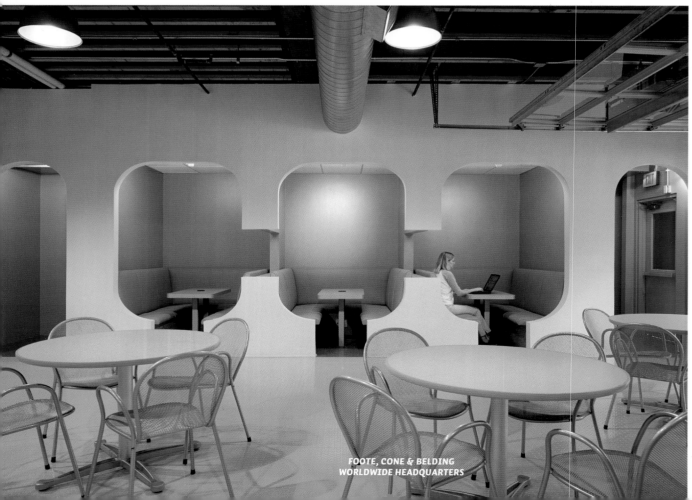

FOOTE, CONE & BELDING
WORLDWIDE HEADQUARTERS

LOS ANGELES DESIGN CENTER

JOHN FRIEDMAN ALICE KIMM ARCHITECTS

SOUTH CENTRAL LOS ANGELES, 2003

Both commanding and beautiful, the Los Angeles Design Center represents a major investment in South Central Los Angeles, an area that has seen little development since the 1992 riots. The first phase of a master plan to revitalize an area where many of the city's furniture manufacturers are located, the Design Center was the brainchild of Cisco Brothers' founder Francisco Pinedo, who wanted to create a public focal point for the revitalization effort.

LOS ANGELES DESIGN CENTER

LOS ANGELES DESIGN CENTER

The first phase involved the adaptive reuse of old warehouses and the transformation of a parking lot into a multiuse space to accommodate events. Subsequent phases will entail constructing a tissue of landscaped parking areas, exterior walkways, and interior passageways that will link a series of new buildings, creating a landscaped pedestrian corridor that will lead directly into the forecourt of the current building.

The entry sequence incorporates vivid contrasts between the transparent and the opaque, the ephemeral and the permanent, and the existing buildings and the new construction. The building is an essay in boldness of scale that uses scrims and translucent layers to establish a sense of unity and a bold street facade. The size of the gestures alone is impressive. In one showroom display, four levels of white flooring slide out from under each other; elsewhere, folded plate-metal stairs empty onto a wooden platform stairway that spans the length of the room.

WEST HOLLYWOOD GATEWAY

WEST HOLLYWOOD GATEWAY

JERDE PARTNERSHIP

WEST HOLLYWOOD, 2004

The West Hollywood Gateway is the opening salvo in the City of West Hollywood's efforts to revitalize the area east of Fairfax. Built on a site where a car wash, a homeless shelter, and nondescript film production houses once stood, it now offers the only opportunity in West Hollywood to shop at big-box stores like Target and Best Buy. Its next phase will involve the construction of three hundred units of housing on the remainder of the block.

The design reflects two big ideas, the first of which is the simplest of urban mantras: create a commercial street front instead of hiding retail away in a mall. The second involves incorporating a protected, semipublic space—in this case, an oval courtyard with built-in benches that maintains a connection to the street life at the gritty, bustling corner of La Brea and Santa Monica, but is removed enough so that it feels like a place to linger.

WEST HOLLYWOOD GATEWAY

On Santa Monica Boulevard, the building's facade has a gentle, concave curve covered in opalescent glass tile. Set back twenty-six feet from the sidewalk, it makes space for a double row of trees, an urban amenity absent elsewhere in this part of West Hollywood. On La Brea, smaller retail stores create a lively street front.

Lighting and landscaping were key parts of the design. A variety of sources—a light tower, fins, and lights on landscape elements—provide pedestrian and automotive interest. Among the most active elements are large video screens used to display public art and advertisements.

WEST HOLLYWOOD GATEWAY

SUNSET AND VINE MIXED-USE PROJECT

ROSCHEN VAN CLEVE ARCHITECTS WITH NAKADA + PARTNERS   **HOLLYWOOD, 2004**

For decades now there has been a disjunction between the legend of Hollywood and Vine and the lackluster reality. This building accordingly faced a much bigger challenge than most: not only did it have to serve as both a place for people to live and a tourist destination, it also had to project an entirely new image of downtown Hollywood.

SUNSET AND VINE
MIXED-USE PROJECT

Occupying a full city block between Hollywood and Sunset Boulevards, this mixed-use development incorporates the shell of an existing streamline-moderne structure on Vine—the original ABC headquarters—recycling it as a Schwab's restaurant (and confounding tourists who may mistake it for the original Schwab's, where Lana Turner is often said to have been discovered). The new building has a relatively simple base with punched openings, some recessed to create an impression of thickness. It has several winningly idiosyncratic spaces, including a rooftop pool hidden behind the ABC facade, which sits next to a stunning, double-height corridor running parallel to Vine. Small billboards incorporated into the building connect it to a Southern California tradition dating back to the origins of the Sunset Strip, as well as to the Melody Lane Café at Hollywood and Vine, where Richard Neutra's 1932 design featured rows of billboards for Universal Pictures along the roofline.

SUNSET AND VINE
MIXED-USE PROJECT

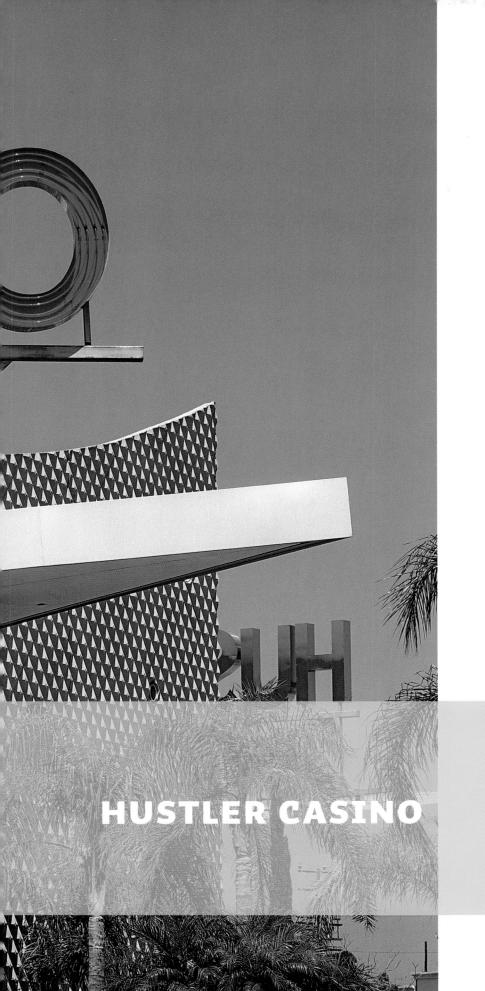

HUSTLER CASINO

GODFREDSEN-SIGAL ARCHITECTS

GARDENA, 2000

Say what you will about porn legend Larry Flynt, he's a guy who knows how to have a good time, and that's written all over this building. It may be unabashedly showy, but it is such a good-humored display of brazen glitz that it provides a nice contrast to the cyber-machine minimalism that currently has an iron grip on architectural fashion.

The idea for the casino originated because Flynt needed somewhere new to hold his poker "home game," an all-night affair with a $400,000 pot he had been hosting at his house. Accordingly, the architects created an elliptical, seven-sided casino with mohair-padded wall panels punctuated by buttons. On the exterior, gold-colored, tilt-up concrete walls of different heights and

lengths evoke the image of a medieval stone structure—albeit one punctuated with round windows and neon circles of light, and embellished with flecks of mica to reflect the changing patterns of sunlight throughout the day.

The stone-and-glass lobby provides a transition between the fortresslike exterior and the soft mohair interior. A hyperbolic paraboloid perforated-steel ceiling with hidden attached panels is suspended from the structural ceiling, and articulated by strips of light where the wall meets the ceiling. Brightly colored coves in the ceiling are adorned with massive crystal chandeliers, creating the illusion of a larger dome above. And because well over half the casino's patrons are smokers, at the heart of the building is a smoking courtyard, topped by a giant lotus-flower-like fabric structure that opens or closes in response to the elements.

HUSTLER CASINO

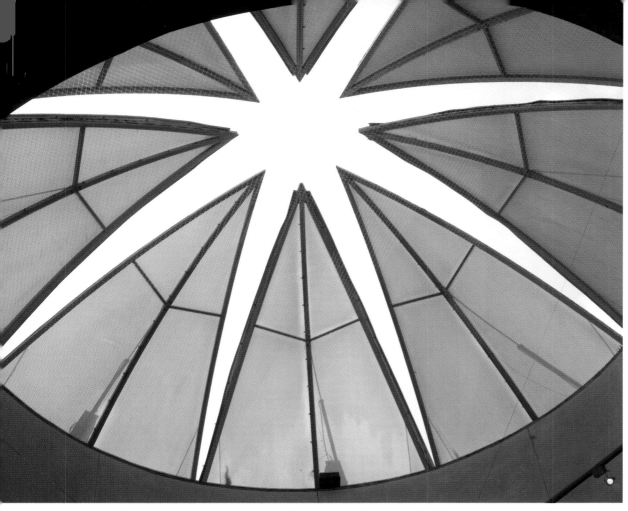

HUSTLER CASINO

THE BEEHIVE

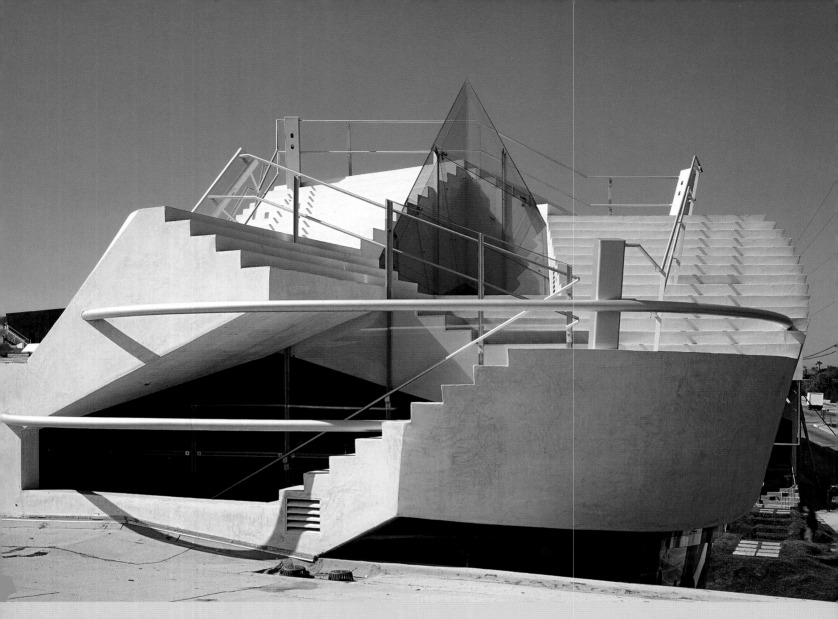

ERIC OWEN MOSS ARCHITECTS

CULVER CITY, 2000

Eric Moss's work in Southern California can be largely credited to a single pair of clients, Frederick and Laurie Samitaur Smith, of Samitaur Constructs, who have given him free rein to create a series of iconoclastic buildings, transforming an aging and decidedly unchic Culver City industrial district into a mecca for creative offices. One of the single most anti–New Urbanist architects in Southern California, Moss obliterates the conventional sense of buildings as boxes and reconceives them as objects that are surprising, aggressive, or confounding. His buildings are about standing out rather than fitting in.

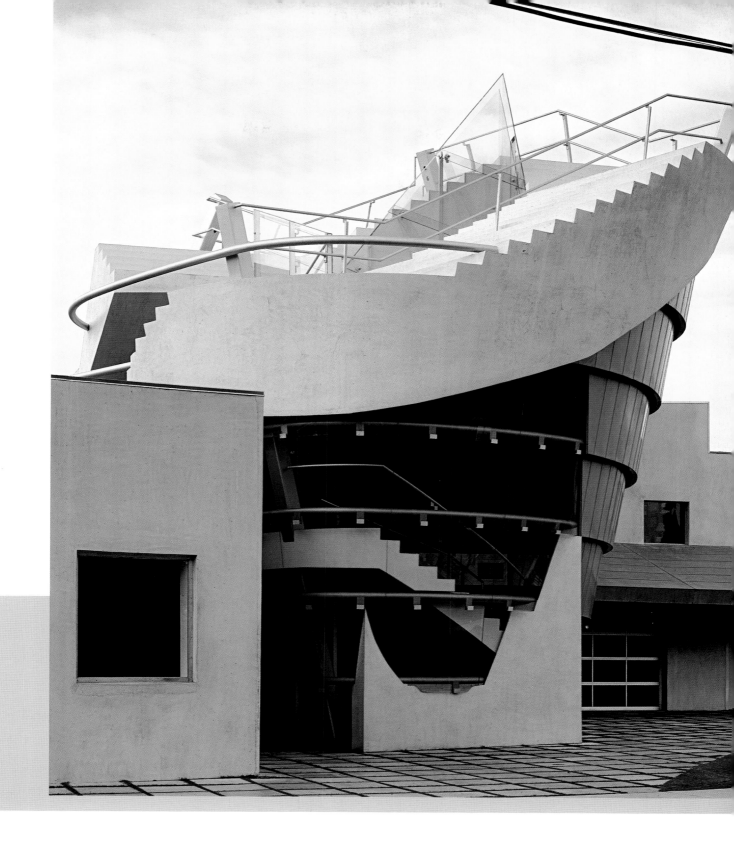

THE BEEHIVE

The Beehive, an office building for an Internet company, is a case in point. Medschool.com, the client, needed lots of open work space and a few private offices. Providing that required partially demolishing an existing one-story building and adding a second story. A section of the second floor was cut away to admit natural light, and clerestories and a central skylight were added.

The building's glass planes and thin sheet-metal walls are visible on the interior and exterior, and its swelling spiral suggests a fragmented version of Frank Lloyd Wright's Guggenheim Museum. A stairway from the second-story conference room leads outside to the roof, where it wraps around a triangular skylight and creates an outdoor conference space with views of the neighborhood. The multiple exterior stairs and semiprivate garden plaza encourage employees to relax and socialize in the landscape, while the beehive form creates a strong presence on a site with only thirty-five feet of street frontage.

SALADANG SONG

TOLKIN & ASSOCIATES

PASADENA, 2000

The most exciting indoor-outdoor restaurant in Southern California—and one of the most lyrical outdoor rooms—the Saladang Song restaurant is a shining example of what can be done with tilt-up panel construction, a technology usually reserved for utilitarian warehouses devoid of architectural embellishment. In partnership with John Raymond Byram Architect, Tolkin & Associates created panels that stand like giant dominoes, poured on site and raised into place. Ordinarily, isolated slabs like these would simply fall over, but here they are held in place by an underground beam.

SALADANG SONG

Thai fabric patterns served as inspiration, abstracted and re-formed into infill patterns between the concrete panels. The restaurant's open glass pavilion is surrounded by screens with alternating solids and voids. (An aerospace contractor produced the laser-cut steel screens directly from computer files, and they are the pièce de résistance of the project—and a bargain at only eighty thousand dollars.) These screens and the other exposed steel elements were finished in a metallic-flake automotive paint and exhibit a welcome—and uncommon—sense of playfulness and whimsy in a contemporary modernist building. The restaurant's owner resides on the third floor, in a penthouse apartment.

SALADANG SONG

SALADANG SONG

L.A. UNIFIED SCHOOL DISTRICT
PRIMARY CENTERS

RIOS CLEMENTI HALE STUDIOS   **LOS ANGELES, 2002**

In order to reduce class sizes for the city's youngest students, from kindergarten through second grade, the Los Angeles Unified School District commissioned prototype classrooms designed to adapt easily to one- to two-acre sites throughout the city. Built in pairs with a common wall, the classrooms have windows on three sides and an inverted roof to make room for clerestory windows.

L.A. UNIFIED SCHOOL DISTRICT
PRIMARY CENTERS

Moving towards SUCCESS!

¡Moviendo hacia el EXITO!

성공 으로 한걸음식!

Standardized support buildings and classroom dimensions (all are twenty-four by forty-eight feet) lower costs, but the project's real appeal lies in its treatment of the landscape as active space—as well ordered as any interior—and in the contrast between the bright colors and patterns and the austere architectural vocabulary. Color is used throughout to animate, differentiate, and identify various building functions, and it serves as a beacon for children approaching from the street. Courtyards serve as extensions of the classrooms, and the central court features a vividly painted carpet embellished with tennis-court and traffic paint. The wall murals were inspired by the bold graphics in the local Latino business district.

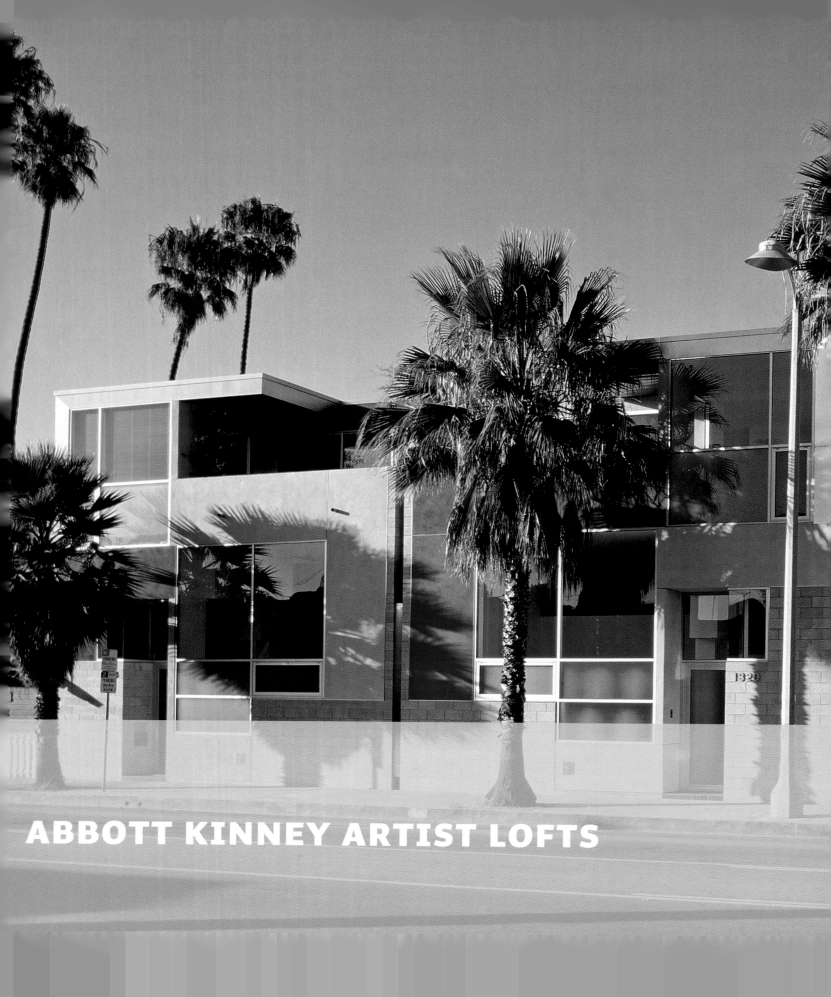

ABBOTT KINNEY ARTIST LOFTS

MACK ARCHITECT(S)

Abbott Kinney Boulevard has a reputation for being on the cutting edge of style and urban living on Venice's west side. It has long been the haunt of artists, but the time is past when there was so little retail traffic that commercial storefronts could be used as artists' lofts. Artists moving here today had better be prepared to bring plenty of cash, as the area seems in danger of turning into an enclave reserved for the affluent.

One of the most obvious signs of the neighborhood's transformation into a high-style retail zone—as well as a coveted residential area—is the burgeoning construction of live-work space and lofts like Mark Mack's project, which consists of three separate town houses on three different lots, blending living and working environments. The units were intended for small business owners, such as designers or film producers, who wanted to work at home. (The clients, a contractor and a realtor, kept the middle unit for themselves and sold the other two to entertainment-industry figures.)

**ABBOTT KINNEY
ARTIST LOFTS**

The three buildings are united with a common palette of bright, warm tones and variations on a theme that determine fenestration patterns. On Abbott Kinney, the windows are frosted for privacy on the lower panes and divided into operable and inoperable sections. In an attempt to create a strongly urban street wall, the architect broke the Abbott Kinney facades only with recessed entries and street-front balconies on the third-floor level. On the alley facade, however, the upper stories are broken into three cubes to conform to the scale of the low-rise neighborhood to the east. The plan locates the work space, along with a five-car garage (parking is famously scarce in this neighborhood), on the ground floor of each unit. On the second level, an open mezzanine and a kitchen–dining room sit next to a double-height interior court. On the third level, two bedrooms are separated by a bridge overlooking the light court.

ABBOTT KINNEY
ARTIST LOFTS

CONGREGATION KOL AMI

SCHWEITZER BIM

WEST HOLLYWOOD, 2001

Congregation Kol Ami is now a West Hollywood institution—a gay synagogue with a significant number of gay parents—but it faced a tricky approval process. The city's zoning code is based on urban-planning doyenne Jane Jacobs's ideas about communication and interaction with the street, and the synagogue needed to offer privacy for worshippers without appearing fortresslike. Architect Josh Schweitzer, who inherited the mantle of stucco-box master from Frank Gehry (who has long since moved on to more diverse—and expensive—materials), came up with a solution that involved peppering the facade with tiny windows à la Ronchamp. Small fins on each window are inscribed with Hebrew letters to make the wall look as if it has been peeled back, animating the building while shielding the hall of worship from passersby.

In silhouette, the structure resembles a pile of boxes jumbled together, culminating in an element that most religious buildings don't have, but one that makes a lot of sense on a cramped urban site—a roof deck (complete with bathroom) that can be used for festive occasions. But what is really remarkable about the synagogue is the way it takes a mundane building material—the lowly acoustic tile—and transforms into a design element.

CONGREGATION KOL AMI

JAI HOUSE

LORCAN O'HERLIHY ARCHITECTS

CALABASAS, 2004

The Jai House is proof that Los Angeles is still producing modern houses as elegant as any that emerged during the heyday of the Case Study House program half a century ago. On a gently sloping site overlooking the Santa Monica Mountains, it is composed of a series of boxes, its walls of glass framed by solid planes. Alternating surfaces of black and white plaster emphasize the disparate building blocks. The primary level, which houses the living and dining rooms, the kitchen, two bedrooms, and a yoga studio, rests

JAI HOUSE

on the earth at one end and cantilevers out over the site on the other. The second story consists of a single box perched at a right angle to the ground floor, which extends on either side. A perpendicular, seventy-five-foot lap pool passes straight through the house, where it becomes part of a polished composition incorporating a stairway with treads hung from metal cables, blurring the line between landscape and structure. There are no extraneous gestures. Equally direct in its approach is the master bath, where tub and sink share space with the bed, reinforcing the general theme of openness.

J. PAUL GETTY MUSEUM FAMILY ROOM

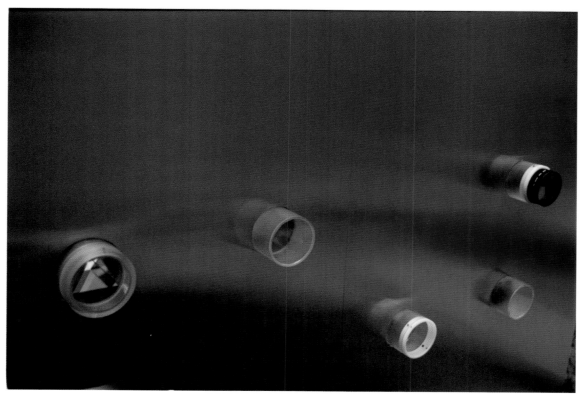

PREDOCK_FRANE ARCHITECTS   **BRENTWOOD, 2004**

An exercise in minimalist art, this gallery for children in Richard Meier's 1984–97 J. Paul Getty Museum resembles a cross between the sculpture of Donald Judd and the color studies of Josef Albers. According to the architects, the family room is everything the Getty is not, "a diminutive, temporary, polychromatic, experientially based room within a room" characterized by a dynamic tension between rigorous formal order and a sense of play.

  Five stainless-steel-covered twenty-foot cubes sit within a white-box gallery; each houses activities that elucidate a different art form: drawing and illuminated manuscripts, photography, painting, sculpture, and decorative arts. The cubes' interiors are flooded with color that complements the artwork on display inside and spills out into the larger gallery, and their walls are studded with peepholes that reveal objects and detailed images.

J. PAUL GETTY MUSEUM FAMILY ROOM

J. PAUL GETTY MUSEUM FAMILY ROOM

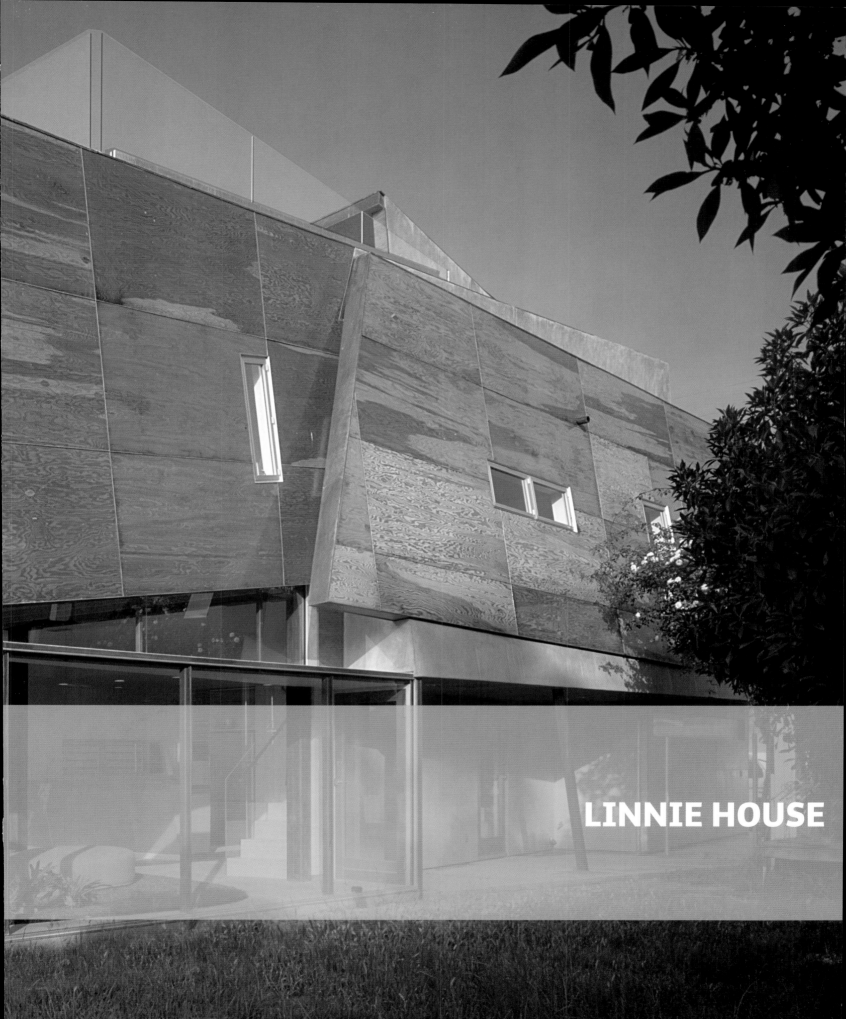

LINNIE HOUSE

LINNIE HOUSE

MICHELE SAEE

VENICE, 2005

Venice is one of the most picturesque parts of L.A., and within Venice itself, the most picturesque areas are the canal neighborhoods. Many of them retain an intimate scale, although a number of the older houses have been torn down to make way for larger structures that occupy as much of their lots as legally possible. The Linnie House has a gentler impact on its setting, because the side of the house that faces the canal is stepped back and almost entirely transparent.

The living room projects out from this transparent facade under a razor-thin roof. On the second story, the glass master bedroom wall is deeply recessed between the roof and end walls. The three-story alley facade is clad in plywood top to bottom, integrating the garage door. All the plywood panels are carefully flashed, with detail that includes mitered corner channels.

LINNIE HOUSE

The clients, a UCLA physicist, Lothar Schmitz, and an attorney, Shelley Berger, did much of the work themselves to keep costs down, including technically demanding tasks such as installing radiant heating, low-voltage electric, and glass-and-tension-wire railing systems.

Saee, who spent two years working for Morphosis, is the most prominent Los Angeles architect to have been profoundly influenced by the firm, as his deconstructed forms demonstrate. Orthogonal lines and forms crash through each other, intersecting and collapsing. The long side elevations resemble a series of colliding boxes, and the house shifts from three stories on the alley side to two on the canal side, with an intermediary loft and double-height space in between, in the building's center, creating the impression of a simple, primary volume shattered by an impact. The house also incorporates diagonals in both elevation and plan; one is the angled demising wall to a separate studio unit, which forms an elongated triangle in plan, with the bathroom at the head of the triangle and the bedroom at its base.

HYDE PARK MIRIAM MATTHEWS BRANCH LIBRARY

HYDE PARK MIRIAM MATTHEWS
BRANCH LIBRARY

HODGETTS + FUNG DESIGN AND ARCHITECTURE   **SOUTH CENTRAL LOS ANGELES, 2004**

One of only a handful of architecturally distinguished buildings constructed in South Central Los Angeles in the last forty years, the Hyde Park Miriam Matthews Branch Library stands at the corner of Florence and Van Ness Avenues. Designed by Craig Hodgetts, a protean creator who delights in invention and cultural commentary, and his wife, Hsin Ming Fung, who brings a laser-like insightfulness to the partnership, it is one of the most successful examples of the city's recent library expansion campaign.

The front facade on Florence is divided into three sections: a boxy volume of copper-colored steel on the east, strip windows over vertical moss-colored cement-board siding, and projecting metal rafters. The most arresting, and original, element is the constructivist light baffle in the northern parking lot—a sculpture composed of glass, metal grating, cement board, and steel—that creates an extraordinarily rich back entrance. The capacious interior has a single volume for reading rooms on the west, opposite a service wing, and is articulated with a series of ducts, lowered drywall ceilings, and raised, beamed ceilings, creating a lively sense of spatial play.

HYDE PARK MIRIAM MATTHEWS
BRANCH LIBRARY

APT
For RENT
(323) 938-7467

HYDE PARK MIRIAM MATTHEWS
BRANCH LIBRARY

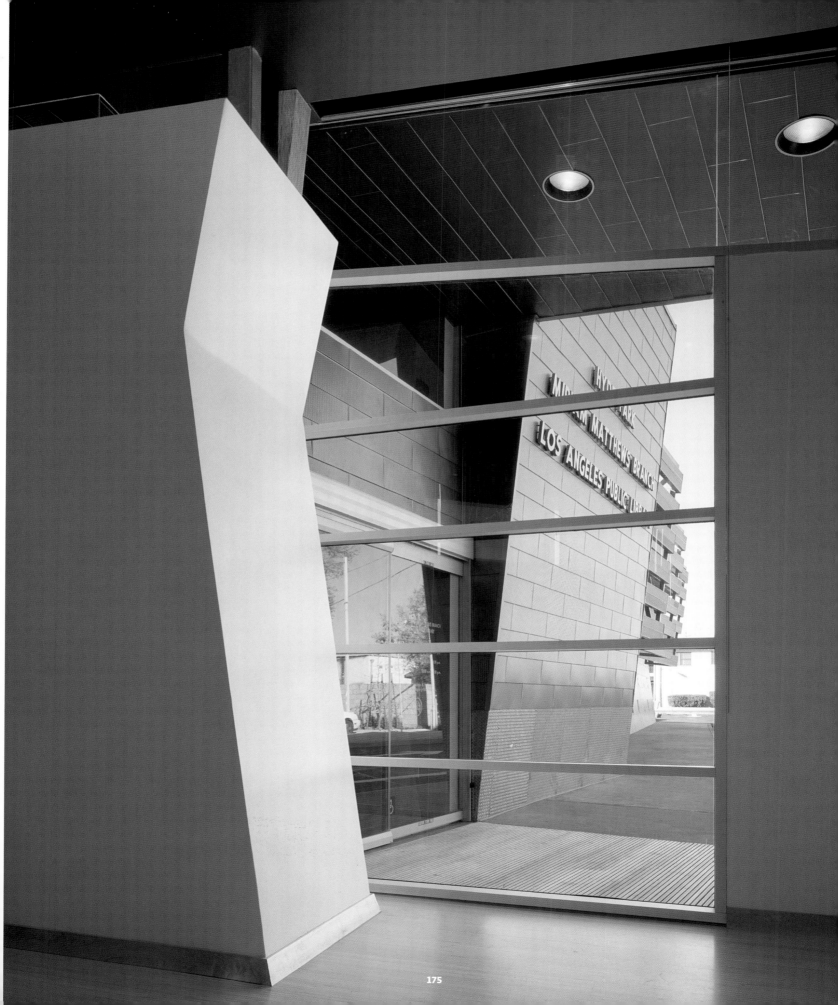

PLUMMER PARK COMMUNITY CENTER

PLUMMER PARK COMMUNITY CENTER

KONING EIZENBERG ARCHITECTURE   **WEST HOLLYWOOD, 2000**

Plummer Park is not just any park—it is an outdoor living room and nonstop kibitzing center for West Hollywood's Russian community. The gay-friendly city is not usually thought of as a place for seniors or families, but they are precisely the constituency the park serves.

For economy's sake, part of an existing facility hidden away behind parking lots on Santa Monica Boulevard and Fountain Avenue was reworked to create a new intergenerational facility for the park. The one-story structure is a true California building,

PLUMMER PARK COMMUNITY CENTER

cousin to a Cliff May ranch house. It incorporates multiple courtyards and has strong indoor-outdoor connections, but it also has elements that make it distinctly contemporary, including a corner clipped off in a Frank Gehry–like trapezoidal shape. Facilities for teens and seniors are housed in separate wings linked by a double-loaded corridor, with shared services in between. Courtyards on either side of the corridor frame the central entry point. Open, faceted plywood ceilings and eaves lend warmth to the interiors, as does the thoughtful and varied use of glazing and natural light throughout. One meeting room receives light from a nearby courtyard, which is walled off from the western sun but open to the sky above; another is illuminated by a large interior clerestory window onto a skylight in an adjacent hall.

PLUMMER PARK COMMUNITY CENTER

RUTH AND CHARLES GILB
ARCADIA HISTORICAL MUSEUM

RUTH AND CHARLES GILB
ARCADIA HISTORICAL MUSEUM

SPARANO + MOONEY ARCHITECTURE ARCADIA, 2001

It's a bit of a shock to find such an austerely modern building in Arcadia, an affluent suburb east of Pasadena best known as the home of the Santa Anita Racetrack and the ethereal Queen Anne cottage where the television show *Fantasy Island* was shot. But this new museum devoted to the history of the region is a clear descendant of the magnificent sprawling ranch houses that proliferated in this part of the San Gabriel Valley in the 1950s.

Simple buildings with absolute clarity of purpose are often the real gems in architecture, and this is one of them. On a lush sub-urban site overlooking a golf course, the architects juxtaposed a brick service-and-office wing with a wood-screened gallery wing, creating dramatic interstitial spaces between the slatted screen and the building's exterior wall. The two wings, which surround a forecourt and covered patio, are punctuated with windows placed whimsically to create playful surprises and provide glimpses of the outdoors.

RUTH AND CHARLES GILB
ARCADIA HISTORICAL MUSEUM

SOLAR UMBRELLA HOUSE

SOLAR UMBRELLA HOUSE

PUGH + SCARPA ARCHITECTS   **VENICE, 2005**

Lawrence Scarpa and Angela Brooks, married architects, transformed a small, nominally Hispanic 1920s developer house by blowing out the rear and adding a two-story, tilt-up wing with space, light, and refined architectural detailing. The addition houses a two-story living room and master suite, and a combined bath and utility room.

The design incorporates a reference to Paul Rudolph's iconic 1953 Umbrella House, which employed a wooden trellis to protect the structure below. Pugh + Scarpa's riff on the concept involved creating a canopy out of eighty-nine translucent solar panels, covering the western facade and satisfying most of the house's electrical needs. Rising a story above the roof, it forms a unique terrace that is simultaneously monumental and intimate, open and sheltered. The elevation that packs the biggest wallop is on the northern side, where a composition of shifting planes and vertical and horizontal beams and posts makes the structure seem more like a delightful tree house or pavilion than a conventional single-family house.

SOLAR UMBRELLA HOUSE

LOIS AND ROBERT F. ERBURU GALLERY

FREDERICK FISHER AND PARTNERS   **SAN MARINO, 2004**

The Huntington Library's sense of design can be hit-or-miss (witness the badly proportioned neoclassical Munger Research Center recently erected at the entrance gate), but its new Erburu Gallery is a welcome exception. The best part of this elegant, sixteen-thousand-square-foot addition to the Virginia Steele Scott Gallery of American Art is the glassed-in loggia along the north elevation, inspired by the Louisiana Museum of Modern Art in Hummelbaek, Denmark, which creates a visual connection with the gardens. The rear interior wall is finished like the exterior of the building, creating a feeling of being inside a giant screened-in porch. Behind the loggia, four square and three rectangular rooms are arrayed around a central octagonal gallery, illuminated by a combination of natural and incandescent light.

LOIS AND ROBERT F. ERBURU GALLERY

The design was influenced by Sir John Soane's celebrated Dulwich Picture Gallery and replicates the lofty proportions of the Huntington's neoclassical buildings, although it also evokes the measured cadences of Mies van der Rohe and Philip Johnson. One unusual feature is a corner clerestory-skylight that lets in a dramatic shaft of light and can be shuttered with a "light cap" when not in use.

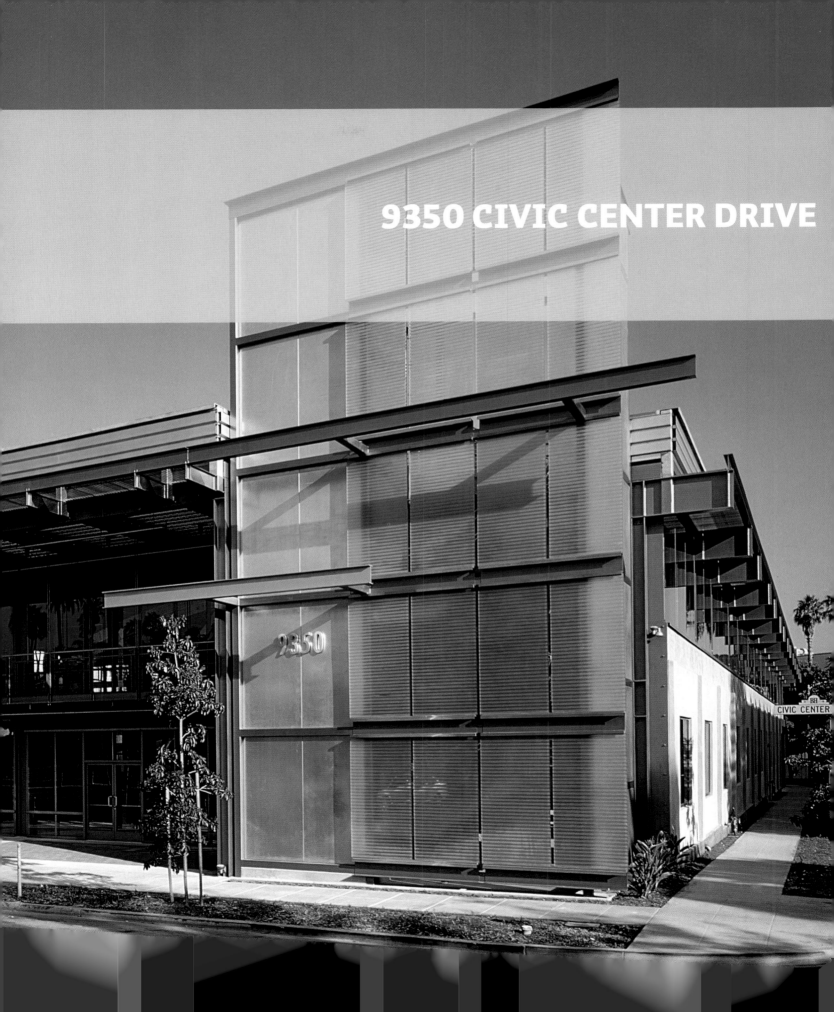

9350 CIVIC CENTER DRIVE

BARTON MYERS ASSOCIATES   **BEVERLY HILLS, 2001**

The elder statesman of urban design in Southern California, Barton Myers preserved half the walls of an existing brick warehouse, not only to imbue the new building with historical character, but also to take advantage of the original building's generous parking and setback allowances. The warehouse had a perimeter wall of unreinforced brick and two sets of wood trusses supported by a row of columns; Myers kept one set of trusses, supporting them with a steel framework and recycling them as ceiling structures in the new building. He also added a rooftop parking deck with a steel structural frame and a new mezzanine, as well as seismic reinforcing for the existing masonry wall. The structure is exposed in all its complexity—steel pipe braces centered on window openings can be seen from the exterior, and the north tower stair incorporates big panels of glass sandblasted with stripes. Its dramatic height on Civic Center Drive creates a monumental portico as imposing as that of any neoclassical bank or government building.

9350 CIVIC CENTER DRIVE

THE WHIDDEN LECTURES

1. (1956) C. W. de Kiewiet: *The Anatomy of South African Misery* (1956)*

2. (1957) Vijaya Lakshmi Pandit: *The Evolution of India* (1958)*

3. (1958) Ronald Syme: *Colonial Élites: Rome, Spain and the Americas* (1958)*

4. (1959) Charles de Koninck: *The Hollow Universe* (1960)*

5. (1960) Sir George Clark: *Three Aspects of Stuart England* (1966)*

6. (1961) W. F. Albright: *New Horizons in Biblical Research* (1966)*

7. (1962) J. Robert Oppenheimer: *The Flying Trapeze: Three Crises for Physicists* (1964)*

8. (1963) Ian T. Ramsey: *Models and Mystery* (1964)*

9. (1964) David Daiches: *The Paradox of Scottish Culture: The Eighteenth Century* (1964)*

10. (1965) W. Arthur Lewis: *Politics in West Africa* (London, Allen & Unwin; New York and Toronto, Oxford University Press, 1965)

11. (1966) Sir Anthony Blunt: *Picasso's Guernica* (1969)*

12. (1967) Northrop Frye: *The Modern Century* (1968)*

13. (1968) Barbara Ward: *The Culture of Abundance*

14. (1969) Hans Seyle: *Creativity in Medical Research*

15. (1970) Sir Eric Ashby: *Masters and Scholars* (1970)*

16. (1971) Constantine Doxiadis: *How to Build the City we Need*

17. (1972) Milton Babbitt: *The Relations in Music*

The Lectures are delivered each year in January: the second date is the year of publication. The lectures with an asterisk have been published by the Oxford University Press.

THE NEMESIS OF EMPIRE

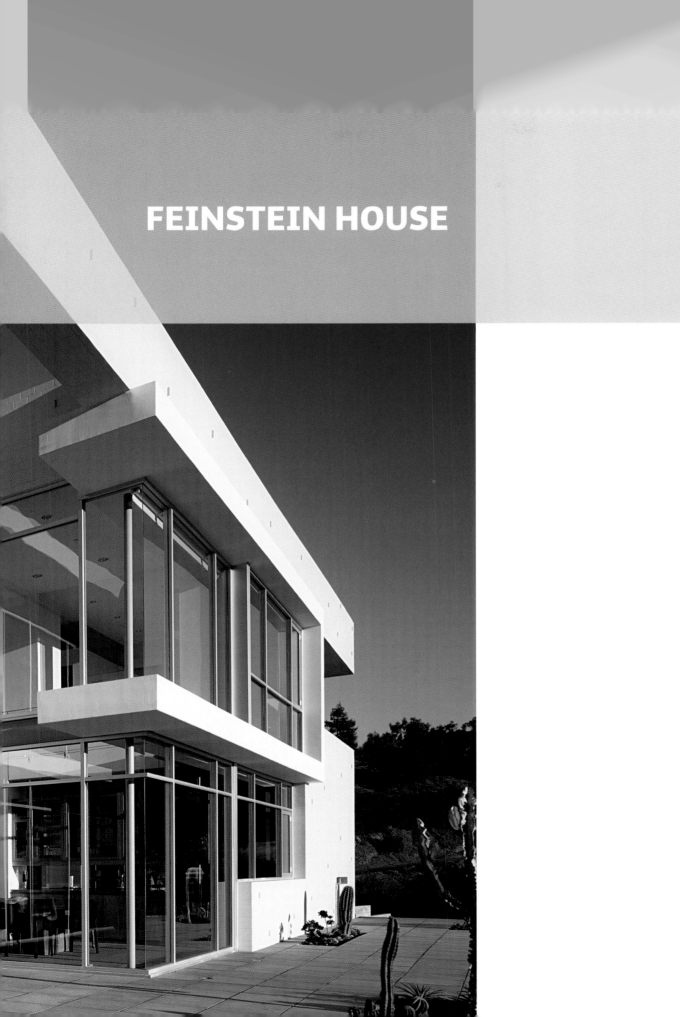

FEINSTEIN HOUSE

KANNER ARCHITECTS   **MALIBU, 2003**

A straight-ahead modernist structure with the horizontal lines of a Richard Neutra building, the Feinstein House was built on a site damaged during the Malibu fire of 1996. The house is set into the hillside so that the second-story rooms on the north are accessible at grade. A bridge and stairway span the entry courtyard, connecting two double-volume spaces. Only twenty-five feet wide because of the long, narrow footprint of the site, the house has huge windows that take advantage of the views; projections on the south-facing walls shade the double-glazed glass.

The client, a dentist, wanted a house that would express the precise, technical nature of his work, so fire-resistant porcelain tiles were used to clad the structure, as a metaphor for the art and science of dentistry. In elevation, the design is disarmingly simple, but it is the depth of the projections and the thickness of the walls that invests the building with character and gives it a heft and weight, distinguishing it from earlier International Style houses in Southern California.

FEINSTEIN HOUSE

STUDIO PALI FEKETE ARCHITECTS   **VENTURA COUNTY, 2004**

The most beautiful structure built in the Los Angeles area in the past decade, the Somis Hay Barn on the Lucky Dog Ranch makes use of a breathtakingly simple design logic, treating the hay as part of the architecture, rather than something merely stored inside the architecture. While hay-bale structures are common in sustainable building, here the walls are nonstructural, serving only to keep out the rain. There are four horse stalls in the barn, as well as room for farm machinery, feed, and tack. Wide eaves help keep the hay dry, and clerestory openings ventilate the barn. The hay walls themselves are intermittently permeable: sometimes hay is added to make room for the horses in the barn and insulate them from the cold, and sometimes it is removed to feed them.

The rich organic texture and golden color of the hay contrasts vividly with the industrial steel post-and-beam building. In a wonderful incongruity, the architects have brought the elegance of the steel pavilion to the barnyard. Their small, perfect pavilion, surrounded by forty acres of lemon groves, is part of a tradition that includes the work of Craig Ellwood and the Eameses, Mies van der Rohe's Farnsworth House, and Philip Johnson's own house.

SOMIS HAY BARN

SOMIS HAY BARN

To my sister's family—
my sister Laura Chase Robinson, her husband, Kelvin,
and their children, Alec, Eleanor, and Oliver

ACKNOWLEDGMENTS

I owe a great debt to the organizers of the 34 Los Angeles Architects show in November 2004; this book evolved out of the material that was exhibited there. Stephen Kanner and Clive Wilkinson were responsible for making the show happen. In addition, Ann Gray, the publisher of Balcony Press, gave me invaluable advice about the book's content and organization. Aiding in the review process of work to be included in the book were Mark Rios, Stephen Kanner, and Jesse Brink, the editor of *L.A. Architect.*

I feel extremely lucky to have had the chance to work with my editor, Noel Millea, at the Monacelli Press. She knows how to allay author fears with gentle positive reinforcement. I have drawn strength from her enthusiasm for this project.

Lorraine Wild, the book's designer, is a design goddess, who has the most refined sensibility of anyone I have ever met. I am thrilled to have had her working on this book. It made a nice bookend experience for me, since the last time I participated in the creation of a similar book, *Experimental Architecture in Los Angeles*, fifteen years ago, she was the designer as well.

Finally I would like to thank my employers, the West Hollywood planning manager, John Keho, and the community development director, Susan Healy Keene, for allowing me to juggle my work schedule in order to complete this book.